Everything, Desire

Everything, Desire

Owen Vince

salò press

This collection copyright © 2017 by Owen Vince

All rights reserved. No part of this publication may be reproduced, stored in a retrieval system, rebound or transmitted in any form or by any means, electronic, mechanical, photocopying, recording or otherwise, without the prior written permission of the author and publisher. This book is sold subject to the condition that it shall not by way of trade or otherwise be lent, resold, hired out or otherwise circulated without the publisher's prior consent in any form of binding or cover other than that in which it is published.

Earlier versions of some of these poems appeared previously in the following journals: *HVTN, Vanilla Sex Magazine, For Every Year, Atrocity Exhibition* and *Fur-Lined Ghettos.*

ISBN number: 978-0-9933508-4-9

Printed and Bound by 4Edge

Cover design by Matthew Korbel-Bowers

Typeset by Andrew Hook

Published by:
Salò Press
85 Gertrude Road
Norwich
UK

editorsalòpress@gmail.com
www.salòpress.weebly.com

For M & D

Table of Contents

Part 1: Marionettes

Everything Desire Is	3
Poem For Pulled Down From Trees Too Early	4
Franz Marc Thinks About The Fate Of The Animals	8
Crater, I	13
Eniopus	15
Zoo Death Contagion Threat	17
Gulch	19
Subjunct	20
Beaks, Breaking The Slight	22
Heat	24
Old Saying	25
Cretan Bull, I	26
Cretan Bull, II	27
Cretan Bull, III	28
Cretan Bull, IV	29
Cretan Bull, V	30
M -	32
Saipan	33
Roofs	34
JJJJ	35
Crater, II	36
Suram Suram Suram	37
Blue	38
Courts Of Glass Buildings	39
Un-Reification	44
The Elimination Of Objects	45
Crater, III	46
How	47
So The Town Square Empties	48
Shapeless Black Dress	51
Agrarian Land Panic	53
Amériques	56
So, Sun Is Conquored	59

Art Histories In Milk Bottles 60
Blood Poses 62
Thirty One 64
The White Sea Baltic Canal Poem 65

Part 2: Altern Modern 68

"*In this country he does not know the word for 'drowning'*"

- Ilya Kaminsky

"*[and] there were no other figures in the landscape*"

- Viktor Shklovsky

PART I

MARIONETTES

Everything Desire Is

        Desire is
        , an " excess
        beyond consummation "

        beyond the neat
        [little] universe , specific
        &c gorgeous ;   it

                is unproductive , the fulfilment
                [of]
                a " beautiful lacking
                of necessity "

"   Everywhere
     it is machines   "

        machines driving &c other
        machines
        &c other
        machines

into what is other than
itself ;   [a vee of grey geese
         slide into the horizon ; my mind goes
        to that horizon ; and it continues
there . . .

Poem For Pulled Down From Trees Too Early

    [is for a body continually
           in pieces , entirely
           in itself , and so expansive and yet
           trapped   it]

[a]
too gathered , the hand is   shaken
     Edge and brought open ;
         [re] worked - yet
         backwards ; how after it , what

is of beauty is firstly
a " foreground ";   and secondly , and gushed
                as mouth ; the Left Hand
                clasps around the Right hand's
                throat -   it Squeezes
   it .

[b]
the too small part [is
     hidden   ; chanteuse , becked plums
     with snow on their
     skin , as
     beneath the much]Other

              ]Just a wround-around
          , loosely to
          hide his

[c]
beach day is sour , too ;   acacia , fallen
                              plums , plastic
    that
    I will not remove this skin ,
    even if my sweat
    rolls down   in   shining
                                  paths ;

[d]
    conscious then , of Lip – or
    sticking together , or
        of
    tongue rolling over
        them -   once , once

[e]
    a landscape [of White Buildings] of , scarred
    part – under thick white white
    heat , as grease ; the body dismayed
    by the mind's desire
    to put it "away"
    from others ;   [S , I am caving]

[f]
the part not wanted
to be looked at is the
part most
looked at
    ; this is a
    salient
    Curse in the
    subject's body – isn't it? And doesn't it hurt
    so badly ? And isn't it
    Fearless , to be impatient   in mykonos ,
your hands swelling
from the heat from -

[g]
when taking Down the body's hold , she notes ;
    the figure stooping to survival
    in phosphate , in 30k pressure,
    in below freezing, in the mouth
    of the desert tunnel in
    buried in Gold ;   as
    for the death mask -   his Agamemnon's face
        twisted in not so much
        surprise as I hope
    Realisation or

what ? Tears for being
a man , and for getting
away with it   for so fucking   Long   ?

[h]

        the three sacred , treasures
    Lost in the Dan – no – Ura
;   green on
    gold , on
    black -

     with these things
     the Body becomes
  un-supine un
   real it
ascends   into formlessness , it will never
     Gesture in the rain , nor
   the lake side nor foreground ;
the Day will have it back.

     [S , my hands are
     still shaking
     ]

Franz Marc Thinks About The Fate Of The Animals

      I.

colour is the construction of the inner
movement of the eye's cancellations –
there are more colours than imperfect
grapefruit halves or bruised halves
of apricot, or closely, the imperfect
continuities
      of folded hooves upon the
wet grass as this animal mouth ; its raised
fact, is caught in the ellipsis

      II.

of itself through tower of shining , as horse
body – who of animal , is retained its
neck leant to'ward the grazed sky in a
sequence
of its geometry – a sequence of adjustments &c
belongings made
to a factory of slow and interacting
objects – i cancel the sun , holding
in my gravitational fingers , blue
off white gloves , a certain eventual sameness of –
the closed eyed
landscape is the afield , of a close

and rushing blue – red – blackened
river ; nothing
    of cuboid horse body is retained , in
    our throttle
    toward disharmony, or trapped dis-

    III.

may – nor is the purple season , with such horse as throat thick
was franz, watching for his lost works dis
grace into the one hundred thirty of their un-
known hander entarteter kunstler -
a mess of forelocks and legs and stomachs and livers
and pancreases and lungs and eyes and mouths and
tendons flowing their movement is wild -
    clicked together feet ,
    grey mouths ,
    black movements in
hamburg , for berlin a craven
room where there is more schnapps ;
Less agitation, as calmly   - once.

    IV.
or wide , coaxial – the important thing
is to keep your hands up the kept-up brush blade
    shifting of his uncertained push those glasses
        upon his nose , in the winter sodden

light or the waiting smoking
brown into which all
shapes are snapped
like bread segments or
shards , sherds of
ice -

V.

shards of red body cubes into another
body , foliates ; her or "mine" / "my" listing my
ship of sense. My sense of "yeah how can
you walk in a continuous
line"
i , myself my discontinue from
the syndicated interact
ing line , sharded tranche
of the sensate world , she grovels throughout
my colour – my wilderness of shapes

VI.

sat before the long replaced square ; canvas , a question
is attached to half-cow-word ; a collapsed shape
as he raises a glass of beer, a magazine, a curtain of
lowing and lowing . the wild blue country is a smashed
duration . the wild blue country is an insistence on
disclosure . the wild blue country is a calculation or

semblance
of twisted daunting, a turned away neck ; "the body collapses
into another , adjacent
body" - desperately sad , - a whorl of strings, hamburg's serene night – the taxis are necklaces, then. His pen moves. The water parts
to reveal

    VII.

men and women in delicate hazel suits – the delayed work ; they grope the open mine's face– they scour for black crystal , which are sunless
parts of horse body or the suspended adze
which sculpted them - "were they not then made by blood and sex?" , and darling , isn't that so old fashioned, even

    VIII.

for the tropic
of westamere , has - a cantering
beyond water ; see ! she held my hand in silence outside the hotel garden . trapped in the discomfort , the suit is too large – the pleiades fell like dropped shoes, they clattered on the pavement
breaking windows
open.

IX.
i'm almost there ! i reach out into the peach farm
trees . his legs are folded , and his hands -
i have "so" many questions , Franz ;
for instance , my name – can you remember
    my name,
        or its meaning ?
           or the hesitance
              of a woman in the blue-lit
                  lobby of the Electricity Board Building?

Crater, I

i dig my Body in
    to it
        , then ; wet clay , Gargantuan [as
        ]   pearling , an escaped
      &c   without
the powered of steel fields , jet plumbed ; only
    years +
years ago before
&c before it – worthless tides as [
reached , reaches and came
sideways] – to bore of machine , its rosy
mantle. twelve unheld
figures , the aerial mast clung to   their passing
faster now and then , slowing ;
tawdry , laughing . Red rose rooms ,
such
    as the pool tables clicked , cake
falling apart   in glass cabinets , &c
everybody comes   for the set
dinner ; passes hands down
, coins on the surcharge – and then went
forwards
      into Ruins ; caked like
        my , mine , mirth , as mad

for its

nape – the tanks that rolled

up namesti miru , into Wenceslas Square ,

&c doused a city ; an entire

City ,

in bushels of unkempt fire .

Eniopus

remember a punching
beneath my nipple, horse
braying – gasped
&c
comes back after
waking to a telephone
    ringing
on this screwy blood-coloured
beach it is barely possible
to grip sand, sandal-shaped things, the bored smear
of sun with all my snatched away finger-tips
    and
    knowing
    of course the afterlife had
    to be pastel coloured and awful
    not because there is fear
    or punishment
    but because
my lust is an endless retreating wave -
it expands
and must contract
into my glutted absurd thighs with my kidney popped
with D-'s bright enormous spear head
    so

I am waiting for a moment
when the sun is less frightening and much fuller
and paints my body on the shore
in reasonable and familiar
colours ; red for key-hole shaped,
the ragged botch
of my death by rapid hard, the kind of knotted place
where my lung was a schizoid almond
and   undone in the bright sanctity
of my chest.

Zoo Death Contagion Threat

the death | of each mountained crystal
lizard triggers
an event of rapid and spreading crystallisation, like the book,
she says, though wavered, with pen tipped
    over 'all crassness,
    was punctuated
    by fear by relevance, that
should you pray now, preprepared - but
the controlled
detonation and riddance
of each poisonous tread each
possibility of continuation. All
sick , as containered &c they were unslouched
but stiffening, like a smell-trigger
    of apocalypse
    wavering toward us, in roadsters, chewing
the tarmac
to pieces, in lunges – with
brittle blashka squid eyes, we said this
is enough is
unquantifiable and has no trace element of irony
or significance ; one mistake
and the world ends
in high midsummer

*when we, | goaded, could not bare
to witness even
a mica [of] frost upon winter windows.*

Gulch

that it is a gap ; the whole earth held
Down ; not by performance its , or first
performative [bridled , it pushed
actually into , soil , wet , brawn
ed &c   1.   Black Tower
, other , other] less > than A -
not , cephalic or asemic blue on
grey grey is on red red on black or
else ; triumphal with air ; the Grace
is not in giving forgiveness it is   2.
recognizing the entire , the family ,
the moire , the split middle ; the
raized hair ; plums , dead on the-silence-of-the-lens
table . Cady for cadence then , dropped
stalls ; the theatre room < or bombarded
with tonic . A bottle slips from his hand onto
    the film reels its uncoiled oil , luck ,
    a belly forced widely
    open ; a red , a depending line .

Subjunct

it de centres ; the ribbon
lost , as
among – quilt chapels , gunwhales ,
arches ; pinewood
forests that run down the country's
side-like
stones ; [they] are forests with sand in them ;
                                            [or]
                    forests with quiet in them , fixated

               between the trees , piles or
               pillars – I walk in to them ;
                                            unless
          fixity , i am held
                    by not being exactly
               anywhere but exactly
               in this position which is
          a denial
          of all positions -   for   taken by
                    missing ; walked ,
                    by gutters by driving rain
                    down it will make entropy
                    harder ; less easy . less loving . L
ess ,

head

strong ; or , quiet -   on a pressed part ,

my pinched bridge

i can see you ;

i can see you , appearing and

still appearing

still .

Beaks, Breaking The Slight

Bird's mouths open ; bird with mouths
open , to asking ; with noise , sudden &c
irregular – birds , with ; streets [along with
    summer ; high on the ankle
    Bone , rubbed – that]

        I gear myself with
           notes in my room ; just , wring
        or pretending to ;

      i don't buy so much as
      Consume ice-cream in the
      sense of luxury ; I watch myself
      eating ice-cream in
a fogged-up shower
mirror where it is so
Warm ;
      in full Knowledge
that Bird's mouth is rotunda , the dome pierced ;
&c reconciled with agape's mouth , tekhne as
soiled , craft – and give you other

as Bird is Bird long , wired , crystalline as
in shopping centres , picking

gum from each
lip ;   not , a very wholesome Bird as
*   bird beginning , its black coffee so*
acrid , without Body ;   and that is how it .

Heat

first , as movement ; glacial , it thinly
as widen , to as ; doors slamming
closed – the iris perturbed , returned ,
degraded ; blowing curtains open
onto   [added ,
                    what is so large-scale
                    in the family is small-scale
                    to the subjection]

    and not , as she was ; occupies
    Every specific contour , a height map , its
    ravaged terrain – obnoxious
    blood ; and then settle , and then settle , and
    then settle
Down into the heart   which has no chambers
    just blood – stretching from wall
    to wall ;   on nights like this
    you cannot count   for stars ;

Old Saying

    the frame dismantled; tangiers
        between hanging , plants
        against the windows ;
          for it is lost   - sons , that bloodied
            with ageing ("how long have you gone
                  , without sun?")
      or
          clouds that
          Gather &c rain
          electrifies
    the maudlin , stillness ; the file
    which collapses
    into the open archive ; it is a sequence ,
    non-hierarchical , w/out practice

            as the Greed i have ,
          as

the Estates rise like arms points out the wavering
roofs ; and in here , a man bent over a silver
        dish ; and in here , a man who shaved
in perfect luxury , with his wrists open ,
and in the bathroom , flowing .

Cretan Bull, I

the many Bull ; was aside as face ,
that
Drowned
in mixed sand – the breath
of hard yellow bright yellow flowers ; the congregation
      of them , in vibrant knots – in
      white bags , caught Like that
      on railings , and so sadly

            [in the province , city , where]

The development of Left-over space ; cubes ,
quadrilant , the sign
of the bull's breast ; a caved-in
Line   as the faucet rusts -
            it stretches time
    + opens red , white , grey
    water into the palms , and these wash
as my face looks away
from the eye   [and]   the Body
            arrives only
            Later ; it dusts itself Down.

Cretan Bull, II

the full force of Haulk ; [bread placed on , bread placed
in water] ; its movement apart . some would say ,

        is how you are supposed
        to gather , for ventriloquy , absurdly
Large , against a background
of wilted almond trees , persimmons ,
never knowing – or caring enough – what the persimmon
   is ;

   the road is smashed down by endless
   forays of Lorries , agile
   cars , hot with flame flame with rouge blooded
   with anklets ; you remember eros , his horns
   crossed , that Nyx was so beautiful , sheathed
   in smoke ; and so bored
      by the conversation she yawned openly ,
showing
      none of her teeth .

        The change loosened , tumbled
        in her palms ; glass with a cross
    of plaster – do not bolden then , or fragile .

Cretan Bull, III

and with [causing] ; He looking out
upon , the rain-smeared   the-silence-of-the-lens
Bull   - diaphragm , loosened
   by   white tie , bossed
        rubber ; the completed halo
           of Bronze .   Agitates into   a slaughter
                                         of the white sleep
                                               bull across

Roads that luck into ; + there is disagreement about
how many you can swallow , and Not then
                dizzy , holding on
                to the cross-bar ; the road
                is a flashing river ,
                and it Drowns you , v.
                slowly

        with yr endless agape eyes ; pearl coloured ;
        scheming ; brittle - - alight , alight or
        wandering   the cross-stitch in Soho ,
        blanketed , near bomb-damaged over-built
        plastic hoarding , lit as if
           by welcoming ;   the dizziness ,
                                         subsides , over most
                                       of the capital .

Cretan Bull, IV

the Dog will dismiss you ; startled , the Bull yet
    anchors itself into the keepsake
    arm – there is body ,
        barely enough , but it is there

beneath a surface ; shied black alight , the field
    of car parts glows &c
oranges in the heat ; is credible or less credibly
awake   ; a glass of what
                my uncles brought me ,
                lemon , white
                Water ;   almost a pain
                to my Lip .

    Bull as brawn ; bull as raced-down
    mass – shied into twisted
        lobby   [as to so as to enter again
                the head as if it were
                a Gallery + the space all white ,
                but just-off , as if sand
                had been mixed] in

    with it .

Cretan Bull, V

let's not play around ,
      "anymore" , as ; the Body is a projection or /
      is projected on by

Violence (others) ; regret (others) ; shame (others) ;
wanting (others) ; desire (others) ; is
an emptied vessel , ,   , only
Name , which belongs
to being reduced &c so remembered

        as struggling ;
     that is an interior thought − reject it .

     What have you been watching lately , on tv , with
      your mouth open ? The mechanisms
     of taking a name away ;

this   meat factory ; how can you watch this
? it depletes , or it denies
you [again , it] ;   partly , though
                                        the forest tips
                                          sideways ;
      Bull (white , soaked) is found
      not wanting but also not

quite dead enough   - they is in the business of rejecting
yr myth ; with their teeth outlining
and the arm held back . As it should be

.

M -

Now   it is morning ; your voice is very distant ,
         and difficult
            to recognize ;   You said something
                  for summer skin , flowers ;
         "the flowers are closed" – up . I can wait.

I want to ,
to go into the town and stand there ,
utterly bereft , want[ing] every
body to reverberate with knowing   -
should I say it?

        it would be easier - "it" - if
        it became normal
        to dump our feelings
        like unwanted fish
        heads ; back , into a churled
        &c pink white sea

                say , say , "look at what
                I've done" ; i have made
                a mess , and it will sink
                into a greater mess .

I am making the earth more sick .

Saipan

the shore bug struck , no sand
    is golden only
    gristle , grisaille , - I mean , not
    White or butter or folded , upon [so archaic , then]
    into [yes yes] itself . like , some
    asinine watered-down ,&c Liver light ;

        i watch the hill brow up
        with trees on it , the mouth
        of the sky ;   helios , burning
                              ; that from here
            you cannot hear what the gods
        scream .

It is a preoccupied thing . I woke again with my fingers
    stuck
    in the pages ; a section , that a statue
    is the endless failure of motion caught
    in the potential of its motion it is

        unrealistic, unrealised desire ;
        never relaxing. So I close the fridge door ,
        with a hum.

Roofs

TWICE – baked , the forecourts
    stuck
      in sun ; motionless with heat -
        the dishes are red clay with black
        glazed innards -   the olives
                      are slick to the touch ;
                      there is lemon rind ,
      also wet , attached ;
moles , a molasses so hot
    it arrives on fire
        [I am dawdling in the imaginary ,
        sun. if there were two of us i'd say,
        what a time to be alive. Harry I can hear
        you from across the rooms ; thousands
        of them , &c how]

      and I said , fuck am I glad you will listen ,
      and that it goes both ways , powerful as it ,
and then
                                                          .

JJJJ

tore into the night ; my breath cold white borrowed air

      -, my hands are still ,
      &c your mouth ,
      and the night as a theme – itself
      a mouth , entering
again the forearm ;

           let's begin as strangers – you walk
           into the sun-cooled square ;

      I will mystify your footsteps ;
      it is a "process".

Crater, II

    a slight , complication ;   the pearl that twists
                                            and spines itself ;
    as
    an inch becomes itch ;
    the walls are itching ;
    they are many fields of marble ;

        photographs then ; of spit
        on flowers -   decide what light to let in
        what to extinguish , what husbands

will go down with themselves (all) , and their pretty cloaks ;

        Med you were so almost a background
        a black coat , singing
        in the heat of Corinth . A burned burned mark.

LOVE is never not
a problem ,   for advanced economies ; it closes gaps,
doesn't it?

Suram Suram Suram

    [A]
I'm okay with this.

[B]
as I am lied to.

    [C]
how there are never , were any risks to be jjjjjjjjjjjjjjjj

BLUE

    on my bed it was , a hushed
    field ;

        on my bed it was a long duration , ***** an
        other stair ;
[or ,

    would the bones be brought back inside the body ,
    folded like clothes
    are folded ?

Just as the stair reaches to Povenets ,
littered
with trash now ;   a small skiff
sways on the shallow canal ,
I hear my own voice echo back at me.

    a man is rising ; he smiles , and I smile.
    We share no language.
        I think we light cigarettes.
      The ferry arrives in two or three parts.

          A dead snake – as long
          as a city – lays stretched out
            upon the water.

Courts Of Glass Buildings

ONE
       " [follow these ,
       to chase your body / into
       language] "

Reykjavik ,
    is brought Forward
    at sundown , and made brilliant there
     as if ; hauled
    into conversion as ten thousand brothers
    and sisters were ; among, a trail of quiet &c
    pleading
    orbs – and then , to Myself
    cleaved - to my skin ; as i went into that
wonderland of Signs , low Gesturing
walkways ; the emblematic fist
of a Modernist seminary – God is found , in a plain and
    white washed room ; st. peter has no courage ;
    i am afraid of finding no bottom
    to this depth ;

TWO

two-storied box flats ; a word , as in ONE
'condominium', i think TWO
that is like 'house' or THREE
apartment ; you think, there are men FOUR
drawing Venetian or Roman FIVE
blinds open onto industrial estates &c SIX
large furniture store outlets ; &c SEVEN
your shadow won't necessarily EIGHT
extend there , for the light is NINE
not TEN
painted on , but 'damped' . ELEVEN

THREE

Dimensionality , the curvature of new architectural tensile structures ; the "twisted body" or
　　　"turning corpse" , transfixes
Malmo's skyline – a body in
the moment it hears a noise, shutting
　　　　　through the ear canal , arriving
　　into
　　paranoia ,

　　　　　and grasping , in the carob
　　　　　stalks ;
　　　　　procedurally,]and so as
　　　　　　　　　forever　　?

FOUR

not belonging , the ford not belonging
    ]in
aware of such folds
in regular
space   nor
the wilted off-black   taffeta blouse
    draped , or fallen
      here and
wait "the one you love
    [is] a mess"

        Wait ;

    iran is an open country ;
    lossless audio formats are
    not entirely lossless ,

        Nor

FIVE

                    to be the least , &c
      so   *hardly*
                          [I can't even , even think]
                 about ; in this briefness ,
folds of [light ...] its
              , Den – the sun a gum
              Ball – the moon a liquid
              substance, resistant to
              meaning . I am okay with this
" *frozen sea* " *– to swim upon its*
              surface
is an epiphany –
mal-adjustment ; basically , that my shoes have
always
been too big. But I was used to that size,
and I bent down
to remove them .

Un-Reification

What trajectory must be left
over, amid the loss
of the centre ; the decay
of the aura ; the agony
of the referent ?   Nothing is quite
                        what it seems
                        at sunset. An orange square,
                        black]shadow falls
                        among the arch[
      es   . To
                        hear the sound of a train
                        arriving. To be expectant,
                        with your mouth still
      &c
                        held open

The Elimination Of Objects

My fire sale
is a soul , unburdened
w. dreamy   eyes ;

    it opens opens , opens

perhaps in the rain   N. London , post
        possibility ; of wanting
that
I was only the fissure
that a ghost remainders
[of] itself -   Knowing
    the Object has no capacity
    to act upon its own
    Body ;

until the bowl
slipped
from her hands -   until
    it slipped .

Crater, III

        Crater , is a building
        Now ;
        it pushes your hands

apart -   and then we came
                home , and you
                were walking
        throughout the rooms with your gold
        dragging on the
        floor - I said , ,   I am still
                                    here.

    You said ;
        I know you are. I know]

How

    could it be ,
    otherwise   ; I mistake the road
        of roses , and what is
            your favourite flower ? Does it grow
        in the mountains? Is it less body ,
    and more head ; filled
    with rain
    Water .   ?   st. lawrence
                      is a city , still ;
                      I heard the dust could
                      obliterate & so ravage
                      the buildings ;

    get yr arms off
    me ; get your pretty roads all
        going one
Direction − into the smoke ,
        post-Clovis   a landscape
and you are   in it ,

                      how far we walk
                      is coincidentally
                      how far we "walk"

.

So The Town Square Empties

> "everything gazed at me with
> mysterious, questioning eyes"
> Giorgio de Chirico

by invitation of special ghosts, the town square
        halves
] at its middle; blankness (by which i mean,
blind spots) are woven
into exquisitely appearing
        bodies -   ] i think
        about these as men and
women, dressed in silk stockings,
and too-heavy
lipstick like old
fashioned lipstick
in films that are not
old-fashioned, but
appear so. He Kisses
her, with his mouth closed. [

        Yes.

                              ]

In the town square there is a manifold
pressure placed upon me to arrange my
experience of half-blindness or infection
in hospital wards
or violence
against my person as a poetics ; so,
there. I have Done. But
    should

i be brought into meaning
i will surely fumble it
into the stars, and let them
decide how i will be spared ; not whether, but
"how". i am selfish.
i do not self-govern
my fetish for acknowledgement
but let it spool like threading
paper, endlessly
between my fingers, until the rain,
the paper, the glue, become a papier
mâché in which i build the head
of giorgio de chirico and ask him
about colour, namely; the colour
orange. And then, I burn
my bridges. The countryside

will be laid to waste. By invitation of my ghost, and his instructions from myself, until I ask you to. Until I ask you to.

Shapeless Black Dress

    a proposition -

if rain were to fill a swimming
pool's
foundations ; a grey and
    potential house
    of upstanding iron, pins ; these have
    also
    gone to rust. As in,
would it constitute a new existence, or
would it eat
into the space of my skin, a dropped glass or
ceramic tile, a breaker's
all evening digging holes
or my way out of them ? Would it mean
the same in
Weather, among too much of its
Orange peel. Like her
Shapeless black dress,   the sound her
    pale dress made
    on a wall-length
    mirror with
    pink plastic earrings, dressing
    slowly -

stacked clinker bricks , or
the building is so patient
before it is called together
and made solid
by invisible gestures.
A series of them,
Falling over
Medicine bottles. Old. Their labels soft.
He walks alongside the fence
and sees wet clay.
He walks to the community college
and teaches the poets of the Russian
post-revolutionary
Before they were
forcibly ; removed
from history.
    Three shoes on the, pavement.
    scaffolding, crossed like arms.
    Crossed With Impatience. says, "a blind face is so
    calm so - affecting". Watches,
    their faces hinged / open. Each second
    of time
    is given room. To graze. A s if it too were

Agrarian Land Panic

"gold" is four directions -
"gold" is capable of resisting
water ; by sinking,
gold denies its own capability not
like a papier mâché head with
its ears pulled sideways . I
    have seen a man gesturing in panic , wildly
    and dropping
fondant from the birthday ; worth , of twelve dead
humpback whales washed up on the banks of the
Mississippi . gilded. they were asset mined
by the minute men of Arkansas , drawing
and heaving. Also , as mines exist in potential they
also exist in reality. a speculation is a gesture made
into a fog , it is the hope he didn't see the shape your finger
made (clue: savagery). the men in silk brown blue yellow
white coats are getting closer . tears straddle their nice
cheekbones ! the chandeliers were an investment .
they clatter nicely, together.

    British products can be drowned in ;
        american products are shining ,
rare and traded for kudos . an "agrarian land
boom ensued in the south and west united

states" . Everything was based on a land
boom , he said , "but , in a fake way".
           You know?
Astor , Girard , Paris , and sixteen
million of their friends whose faces are , yes ,
triangulated and exchangeable . the nation's
credit was a gold philosopher blond mega
fauna that screamed over the newly recovered
cities of Atlanta , Chicago , Kansas
and drilled into the asphalt of Minneapolis !
           Mining sounds
           like a rearrangement
           in the language
           of

your listings like -

           this cow creamer is worth
           fourteen of your cow
           creamers ; this oesophagus
           has no exchangeable or market
           value ; this carpet was once
           tailored by the elite carpet tailor
           it is that colour for a reason
           this field is a deflated
           balloon but crops cannot grow

there , or grow all
over the place like
snagged teeth – their sprayed
open corn tastes
yes of glass ; i will see you again
on WS, yes? i will bury my face
in the carpet and meet my departed
dearly friends.

Amériques

so , Desire is a reflection ,   a
   pool of   still moving
      water ;

in the airport line I thought ,
her legs are
exactly , halving
my thoughts ;   they stuck to me like
I walked in the sun . No discard. It is too un bidden .

    [you are a voice that is not reading
    from a script]

      in the airport line I thought ,
      there is an age
      where the buttons simply
      open , and the skin
   calms ;

[now I am tying to find you
across a large container . I have lost your
reflection , because
– this bar is all mirrors. Nobody
  – notices it]

the sirens peel away ;
a death has occurred or
has not occurred

what I mean is that life
is unpredictable
and
mostly sad ...

[my goodness but
you are far away]

I want to reach out in
the sumpter water ; the watered-down
rice wine vinegar , , do
do not drink from the tap . It brings silence
into your body.

[I watch the ten
thousand figures loom
aboard Kronstadt !]

that haxan cloak is
pretty on u

        these are my
        wilderness.

                As .

] what I mean by dissemination
is a critical practice . You are not hyper
vigilant. The bbq party we went to was filled
with strangers. I got drunk okay I got drunk and
kissed him]

                these are stars ;
                I hate them so much!

    When you are alone
    in the fields of succulent
    green stemmed flowers ;
  your teeth growl , + then
  you wait . So you wait you wait wanting
  . these are my

        decoloured things ;
        hemmed away by
        gloriously summer it]

Breathe.

So, Sun Is Conquored

    not invincible ;   *Q , for*
    I take my glasses off , black
    rims ; you kiss
    my mouth , but

        from the side .

So the air empties
some .

        Later , I
        Explain
        how NAME created an installation
        in which the model lay in a
            bowl of almost
        blood-coloured honey ;
        they breathed the air
        through a pale tube ;

I close my eyes
on you. Most of the time
i'm excessive . [it's like that ;
trees ; paint-thrown down clouds ;
                hotness . Hotness]

    and suddenly , the   *it just*
begins .

Art Histories In Milk Bottles

[a]
colour , his

first as wild [to] scurry, raw red ; a mess of immobile
blurring – it works on paper , his years , like blotched '47
too irregularly ; knees bloody from falling | + over ?
Or Read, saying you were dismantled "MAN", car
goed like, heaviness; the man's heav as; unheavenly
body – learn to speak [for] the forest of doubt as white,
unused to bleeding ; a purposeless machine from which
i ; damsel keen, an enchantment of a broken | FORM,
which has no continuities, and is the French word
for "dire", you say it with your mouth , full of sand.

[b]

a glass of milk in which my face is reflected becomes
the glass of milk are blossoms / in which i the milk
was glass centimetres in the pale of montmartre d/
awn was the glass as it folded around the lampposts
of the sahel gorgeous in her infinities , OYSTER
CATCHER COLOURED was or ,the disdain of lips from
ship prows she was the glass of milk i rolled rolled agai

nst my forehead in the book of Wassily K. the substantial assurances of geometry, which become implicated in transference, the serene departure; as glowingly. And as sure.

[c]

(after Andrei Bely)

if we consider only this sequence of (one) clear or shapeless colours and (2) colours (mud, orisen, bluepink), of the ordinary spectrum then (3) colours derived [from] the body, milk, those colours i have rolled against my forehead throughout my veins ; of those bear-coloured, rose-shadowed the buoyant lake or the chiselled pearl held , in the bathwater of grey light ; and only consider the descent into (4) impure colours such as olive-brown, grey-white, formlessness
.

Blood Poses

"After Francis Bacon's 'Three Studies for Figures at the Base of a Crucifixion', 1944

I.
the air is a sexual organ – it carries] disease , dishevels
with its fluke the dry grass around gethsemane where
now there is a fuel station, a triad of white flats , washing
pitched into the sun ; the shoulder blade is too a fluke ,
my bent red intestine – purposing is why I remain, gathered
into segmentations , or else prized out from march , its
worrisome air ; I will wait until my name is called, gently .
This is the certitude I have.

II.
rainbow bird spotting – do you admire the curve of her wing,
its drooling mouth , its horrendous eyes ? in pyrimidines
I call out to the father , say , what is this body in
the air, dropping like a knife into the world's
skin ? he answers, but neither
is this more clear . the world shudders , as if
space has thrown back
one of its own, and he was a tide which sung , and startled
the hemisphere . red black , red black , red black .

III.

a mouth open , as far as ; surely &c this
is night , the clock tower of the furthest point ,
like a scratch made intolerable
on the dutiful skin . Brushworked , that you
get a certain love from sweeping the tiles , your
black coat, the dog's hair, the sky's throat . you
have to press your ear up very close
to hear the scream that caves make, that any gap or breach
in the world makes − just because it's
open − just because you need to .

Thirty One

    I love the city ; its pulverising
    Grey of upturned tree
    roots, its metastasising genres of blank

        ] plastic , its plants
        like obsidian or fragile
        glass wafers that, gently I
        reveal myself to
            its
        calamity – standing , beneath
        the brick arches
        of Holloway] my hand
        clasping a bland pool , an
accidental &c fallen flower , deciding how
to comport myself , how
to wear black
            outside
                of funerals .

The White Sea Baltic Canal Poem

[a]
an empty curse ; with soiled white
hands held – open in prison's
river , forgotten to everything ; even
our anticipate mothers , their remembrance

on the first morning when our sentry
called into the blankness , said the blind fields
were a bounty
to the knowing – such a man mistook the clouds themselves
for bewitched upside-down boats , their pale oars
stroking the nether sea
like cigarette smoke – the wind a smoker's breath ,
our hardness -

[b]
you want to believe good news , or
kill it
very early , before
it sprouts leaves or disperses seed
in the minds of a population who have abandoned
wellness -

[c]
a bird wheels
above the mud pack
river -

I bend my head to see it ;
my neck cranes
sideways -

[d]
sorrento leans into the sea -
the peach white sun leans into the sea -
your cough stifles the sea -
your dead friend , gumilev , is a name in bronze -
they shot him in october , or at the end of september
; sorrento is a wilted forest -
; her squares are sun touched , unlike
the catacombs of lyubyanka, the farmyard smell
that death has

[e]
the stairs of povenets
ascend to death , to subtle
Waters
in the land's mouth – there .
they do not deter me . i am so, so patient.
    &c will I see you there?

PART II

ALTERN-MODERN

*"then cupfuls of
white flesh were thrown
against the building,
its texture
partially translucent -
like a ship's prow
cleaving the smog"*

*TBD
common era, twenty twenty nine*

> "a duration ...
> Destroyed"
> Gaston Bachelard

[s.q]
in sliding his hands across the table into her hands four
hands were reflected on the velum table. A red balloon
coats the winter tree's
branches. A red balloon's skin remains above
the tarmac.   Helsinki
wintered an explosion in its wounds. Its wounds that
were openly
talked about. Its wounds   [that
were openly talked about on talk radio.   as   ]
He slides his hands
into
her   open
mouth, as words fell out
of it. That which opens to swallow galleries which expand
their Golden
rooms. These catch light, on our naked arms, filtering
them, as we rise
      and continue reaching -

[s. j.]
Empty stages to catch, for yield of modern ; it is MASS, with my skin
      as
            . Naturally, there is grass growing between the aisles of the soft-service ice-cream parlour of the vocational
butcher , and
going   He slides
his modern   [   ] into scented myrrh , scents the oblong rig which
      circulates
exaggerated , strides . I asked its body above my mouth's colour,
a thing as   Dire
as our heaven − an abandoned , modernist hotel - its stairwell
drowned in wide and white
clay steps which light spills into , that it makes everything appear "Deeper" - we smear it to the skin
      around
our necks , hoping we'll wake up with love renewed in our hearts, like Vermeer as a girl's
mouth and his sun had erotic slipped its bounds and made this blue alternating, light. Like the wind. He slides his mouth into the mouth. The table reflects three hands. The

other is clasping.

[k.j]
Killwhale , its carcass a pneumatic white
unending ; this was a least expected thing to gain
the ocean , and then
to die here, to run aground ?} i cover my neck in crinoline and
black paper. this is the least I can do, perform
like Hera watching the entire humanity of soiled others
        struggle
among spider , horse , disappearing swan – such
were our heartbreaks , watching from a sun drenched
        country
how york minster unravelled into orange-coloured light ,
and drowned there .   but last night I came
to my senses , still dressed like a roman! we ate pizza
bianca ,
without sauce or colour , in the limelight of that
wounded city . like this you pray for barbarians
to arrive - over that vale , bearing stone , with their
swords drawn.

[j.w]

what is this exactly , another northern sea? its mouth
salt bound its cities are cold
        Gabled
grey rose but for their arraignment of cranes
like noose stalks , even you
must enjoy the subtle water its calming effects
on birds, the absence
of orange peel , litter or overfilling
hospitals or emergency surgery in the culture's
wounds - all of its everything
which survives there, in phone booths,
along shop-fronts , are your mouths in the moment
they are opening , as they begin to draw
in the air. As the words that form. As, as, as, as, as, as

[0.0]

the destroyed gables, above sleeping women that hang their faces
turned are toward Ghent, or the herring
sea, with sporadic gun   fire lifting
the waves ; a wave crashes , or steel adjusts the
smeary air, the saturated canal which suckles on it | all
as if it were a dead-drink, dappled, a sand-coloured cocktail,
or the smell beaches have | in winter, after the drowned
have occupied them, and made them home.

[o.e]

> "I've been paying attention
> to the sky again"
> Stephen Dunn

pirouette, after Jutland, in the ice-crystal sea, the cloudlets for very southern men | in dragged purple coats , or those thoughts you have , about crucifixion, in church ; wondering, did it hurt, and how much byzantine gold can you swallow in a single sitting, stolen away | in flanders, and the grass is very dense, almost black – it contains no nutrients, scoring little lines across | very oblique horizons.

And I wonder about that – your death
of architecture? tarfuri with his head
bent over the cantina tables. Expos. Teori e storia.
    but you didn't retreat, did you?

[a.o]

adjustment music | as in , the school of architecture and planning, on a bygone street, has plenty of glass and a candel-
abra without power, just yolk-coloured bulbs these little gasps of light. A challenge to the darkness | from which city strangled
comes up, jasonite, very scaly, and cannot be your home no in its limelight your paces lengthen and bones quake ,
or quack,
like you confronting fear, amazed by it.

[j.r]

the chilehouse in hamburg morning is hanseatic black - is
a doppelgänger coal but still she will kill her cigarette
on its doorframe, in kissing her soldier husband
>*Goodbye*

as she did a century ago , before he drowned
in arras - &c connected with
all the sybaritic bones , the herring skin , the
house's wattle - for
he was a godly man , six foot one high and had a jaw
like bearing strait his teeth were ship's prows, very
steady.

[d.e]

across flat coastal plane he drives cars, at calais, and gazes at night
with his boot-load wine watching the bonfires of the jungle , lights up,
and the sky has an erotic bronze beneath the car radio is stuck there
will be no insurance money. Gladly, god is on his side , or on the side
as my face is windswept and i call her from a payphone (when
did anybody last do this?) , and my missive is love , it is fleet
and makes great pains to say, "i miss you"

two shining towers. three grey turbines. An axe, falling.

>"what they do is
> monetize air"
> Michael Sorkin

[e.z]

very passive cattle and fish and chip smell as the countryside gives over to scrub and yellow flower , as wind chopped trees to find later there is sand in my hair , remembering how to sip beer in luebeck i was trying to quit , and made idle chat with one of god's own philistines his were very thin grease wrapped cigarettes and the town square was very, he said,

"civic", meaning it was fundamentally all bone, as far down as you can go ; beyond the permafrost , beyond caspar whose paint brushes

are clasped in his hands , he can no longer paint the sea – it has evaporated.

[f.g]

muted saint colours are, generally pearl - like my luggage cases too are worn inherited
cardboard and have the pretence of going from train platforms
the embarrassed sense of time when the train is delayed and you
are hanging on is now , a good time
to leave the country or head into the mist shrouded beckoning beyond
yes there are my people ; DIY creative space or light industrial
units turned into cultural spaces | I sip wine and think "hey", this is very different
from basra or iraq nobody is trying to kill me I said nobody is trying -   hey Viktor S your laces
are undone.
But he didn't hear me -

[d. q]
watch a film with my girl she takes many more photographs than i
do or am capable of she sees
      the world differently it is certainly
a talent when she notices michiru rolling her body like a sea pulls down
the first aisle of her white unmarked leotard across the sudden
unexpected rose of her nipple it becomes this , a coin sound first
into mouthing 'yes' before it disappears into koolhaus junk space and you arrive there continuously in a very nearly identical place , your hands
still wet , and everything – or fixed to an unwavering point like a shopping centre stripped out and the alarm sounding not once
but several times like things that get into your ear and Just.

[e.q]

prairie oyster , a mothership

sized monument

to disadvantage or its misspent

youth around the backs - of places , tides , +

    more

        recondite and surly than alleycats like

her f - ,

madam on a gushing &c parisien street the rain

came down on it with

indifference and my beer , that too [was] warm

and washed down not even quite

the gun metal taste I had there , in my

mouth , and moved around -   it was

shocking , a really shocking time .

[p.u]
over one hundred were in that oilfield , -   ready to return
fleshing home , to retain the holiday sense of life watching the
          chilehaus black
stone become the world's colour , like krimhild's calm and beautiful
revenge it was , he said , 'all very bavarian', and like that it was soft ; my dreams in this sense were a glade , and lang stepped
back
as the body of the true maria raised her arms over the animated
waters and his trousers were folded beneath his knees but you could tell
this was a good time for him , that you can get a taste for drowning cities.

    ["the purpose [is] to impart the sensation
        of things as they are perceived and not as they
        are known"
        v Shklovsky   ]

[s.w]
this has scent ; the   contemporary
                                Bronze
shelter , like hands ; as revolving around
        other
hands , they are holding and beholden like you
have never worn before a mouth mast , a pearl , a marling
on your shapely fears – my fears are fruit in curing
rooms , bound by paramilitaries , concentrated by
ovulating
sunspots in this glare I will be held and made to spit out
my blackburn sins like the shore of iron , the shore of
adamantine
locks where these were the boats arrayed in storms ,
and made to float
in triangles , to lounge in pirouettes.

[z.u]
the consequence of a prurient]as world. as sounds that also constituted
      wounds. Medicine, yet going one. LAX orchid blood
,
      as it Folds ,
    and precariously
    at that .
A bulb hung in the writer's room. It cast light on the silent
awareness of the [face of absolution, a thin night dress slipping the nail along the] white egg - skin body , in perforated to
crack,]under nails, in this looseness.
      [
         , a moment - then

In everything that subsumes.
we climb the staircase. We climb
the windows. So
we continue.
He slides his hands into the duration
of where his hands still lay, on the table, among broken china.   that

      Two hands lay across the table.
      They are upwards facing.

Owen is a writer and digital artist living in London. His previous works include *The Ardift of Samus Aran* (Fathom, 2016) and *Pavilion* (White Knuckle Press, 2016). His digital and performance work includes *'404 recurring'*, a digital installation, and *'1,001 black suns'*, an ongoing photography series exploring 'digital ghosts' within Google Maps. He tweets: @abrightfar